Oubliette
(n) a dungeon with a door only in the ceiling; a place you put people to forget about them.

Dedicated
To the version of us before the storm.

The fabric of our soul before the tear.

To you and I before we know any better.

To the outsiders on the inside.

To my mother for always being there for me and to every stranger I've met these few years that has listened to my side of this story.

Oubliette
by Avery Lynn

However this book is to victims, it's not to the victims who are assaulted. This is to the victim that was the friend. The bystander who got pushed into the center. The friend of both the victim and the abuser. Few to none of the people that read this will understand where I come from or will be happy with the words I will string together. My love for both sides put me in a pit of injustice and grief and I'm hoping this finds at least one of you well. These words burn hot on my tongue because they are so tragic but the taste is bittersweet, because I finally have found words to fill the long pauses I had when this all happened to me. And I laugh because how selfish it is to say "to me" but I won't apologize.... because it's true.

Breaking Point

I watched your eyes sink into your face one day at a time.
I watched you disappear day in and day out — till you perfected your skill of shapeshifting.
One thing I realized shapeshifters do, they convince themselves they are unstoppable.
The reality is, they begin to get messy.
Slipping in their true selves, letting others know something isn't right.
The defense arrives, the anger surfaces and all of a sudden, all at once, they lose themselves completely.
Becoming the monster, they didn't intend on being.

Based on True Events

You will never understand her like I do.
You will never understand what was done.
To hear of tragedy is one thing.
But to have a seat to a show you didn't know
you had a ticket to,
and to watch the story unfold slowly in front
of your eyes.
I tried to look away, I swear.
The only ones in the auditorium seats were
God and I,
and He peeled my eyelids open every time I
refused them to see.
You will never understand.

You weren't invited to the premiere.

Warning

I feel like this needs a trigger warning.
It's a warning for people who loved a narcissist.
Who invested time and effort into a loved one who lost themselves in sin.
The domino effect of tragedy is about to be as real as when you run too fast in the kitchen,
hit your hip on the table,
and spill the drink all over the place.
You watch it overflow onto the floor.. while the pain in your hip is just as prominent as the frustration of the situation.
At the same time I want you to feel bad,
I want to be pitied.
I kinda feel like I deserve it.
Why can't my eyes dry up the same way everyone left me out to.
I guess it's something you never get to find out.

These are just my feelings

Ugly Truth

Sometimes I write to remember myself—to find myself. Because sometimes this world just changes you into something you don't want at all. The only way back to yourself could just happen to be your thoughts you don't turn into words and your hand that fears what will come.

?

Have you watched her change lately?

She's ending each sentence with a question mark as if his response is the answer.
Have you heard her voice slow in conversation as her eyes catch him across the room?
As if his presence steals her breath.
Have you seen her act differently lately?
Her showers are longer and she's canceling on me again.
I miss her smile,
she's hiding his breath.
I miss her laugh, but she's counting the windows and doors, she's too distracted to hear the punchline.

Have you watched her change lately?

Victims Curse

You spoke with such birth, every phrase bloomed a garden.
You chose what to say from what you were taught,
and wrote a script from your inner voice which was his.
When you spoke of love, roses grew.
When you spoke of desire…
lilies, bright blue; yellow too.
You spoke it out loud, no matter who.
You were addicted to the taste.
You never meant a word you said did you?

Too Deep

So weird trying to find things to write about to connect to this story I'm trying to write.
I could write about how I never really liked the burn of alcohol in my esophagus, but became close friends with it being exactly the same pain it felt in my throat as it was in my heart.
How I never felt negatively about myself, till the words of someone I loved deeply said something that hurt deep enough, where it left a scar too deep to heal.
How I could never delete photos because memory was far too important to me, and now I'm disgusted by looking at your pixelated face next to mine... thinking how the hell I let you into my life.
I delete. I delete. I delete. Till my energy runs out and I have to save the rest for another day.

Punching Bag

How can you compare the man who took the most from you, to the friend who gave the most to you.. when you needed it most.

Eve Was A Snake

It wasn't what you wanted to say. It was about what you said, how you said it, and how you actually meant it deep down. You released the snake that was in a cage in your closet of dark thoughts, and it came and inserted its venom into my bloodstream. It made me cold. It paralyzed me. It's like you went to the file labeled "how to suck the life out of someone" in my hidden box of documents of ways to hurt me the most. And you knew exactly what you were doing.

Delusion

You laughed. You laughed? Saying I think of you as evil when you are not, is exactly what the sad villain would say as their back story yearns for them to finally make a hero out of themselves.

Scapegoat

You know you are just like him. Just like your former master. The puppet becoming the puppeteer. An inheritance perhaps.

Which Is My Stop?

Betrayal happens once. the fear of it happening again, breathes on your neck like someone too close on the subway. Hand right above yours, holding on to what is keeping you safe.

Testimony

My testimony happens to be caring for two great people, that were great till they loved each other. And being the only one who gives a damn about what happened. While they both move on and get lost in distraction.

Trauma Dump

You put a usb in yourself, transferred all your **sad**
and gave it to me as a gift.
You suck. You know that,
You think you healed but you actually gave us all
your shit
And left.

Doctors Orders

The disease came. The appointment was arranged. The pre-op was ordained. And the surgery was performed. Yet somehow there's this infection taking place? Every conversation just has to include you. I want you gone but my therapist tells me I have to feel this fully, what was done. And that means you linger in my life, which makes me hate my own.

Forgettable

You put me on life support and the pulling of my plug depended on if you completed your mission or not. Who gave you permission to be God, your freedom wasn't supposed to be my cause of death.

Misunderstanding

It was never victim-blaming. It was character-blaming because of the way you spoke about what happened. I thought victims hated the taste of what was done, yet you couldn't get enough.
Call it a misunderstanding.

American Girl

flowers watered and potted to perfection,
The bible opened to kickstart the days.
I hope you know, you didn't deserve what was done.
you know this isn't something you could've prepared to defend yourself from.
The stories never focus on the good ones.
—the ones who pour the coffee for others, push the children on the swings.
I'm sorry the story was about the pressing against church walls in secret.
The gliding of his fingertips on her palms in a passing of a hall.

fuck them all,
Happy endings are what should get the applause.
not the attention of courtrooms and steel bars.
Not the truth from an elderly lie, a lie that lived a full life—went to carnivals, had lunch, spoke of kids and wedding dresses. I don't want to hear the truth from lips that shouldn't have kissed, or see a hand on the Bible finally telling it as it is.
That bible.
I hope you still open it without having to be reminded of souls that can lift a hand in the second row of a chapel, to also lifting it in court to swear the truth they hid so well.

Graveyard Keeper

I think we ask the wrong people if they are okay.
Okay wrong way to say that, I mean, kindly, we keep
asking on the wrong people—
we forget to ask the boy who can't handle thoughts
of hurting himself without, him.
We forget to ask the girl, who wanted to learn his way of
doing a skill.
We forget to ask the friend that had no friends, except
him.
He has a graveyard of people killed in his name but
the people in charge of the tombstones left too many
without names, too many still uncovered.

The Full Package

You made her think you were a teacher, mentor, father, big brother then lover. You gave a whole new meaning to being the full package.
When she finally realized what she had opened, she gave it to me to throw away.
Without resealing,
Without consideration,
I unpacked and sorted for her.
The recycling bin was empty.

Hidden Places

How dare you use my home as a clinical trial.
Gliding the rough of the bottom of your heal,
up and down her thigh.
hidden where we couldn't see.

I saw you.

Shapeshifter

You were so good at what you did. Until you weren't.

Swimming For Four Years

With the way I'm feeling, I just want to tear open my stomach and tear all my insides out. I want to slam the indescribable mess on the table in front of you, to just look at. To see what you did to me. *You selfish fuck*. All the pain you made me spiral into.

    But that's crazy, right?

To me I feel like it might be crazier to just sit with this anger and rage and let it swim in the walls of myself.

Kingdom Not So United

Everyone keeps saying, "why are you so hurt by this, it didn't even happen to you."
    How do you explain to people the pain and hurt of all the kings horses and all the kings men, when they had to watch humpty go through what he did and have to try and put him together again.

Oh how much I trusted that wall.

"MOVE ON!"

It's funny now that I look back. Being told to just move on, when I was the one you locked in your briefcase of details. You made it my business.

If anything I was squished between the gruesome and secrets whispered, trying to organize, sort the papers you shoved in with me.

As you discarded each bit of trauma, I was still left bleeding out from the paper cuts.

Pity Choir

OF COURSE I WASN'T COMFORTABLE?
OF COURSE I WAS ANGRY?
Why would I believe you, that God would be okay with letting the fallen angel back on stage just because others felt bad?
I guess I carry the wrath and fiery side of our God on my belt, and have a lack of grace and mercy.
It was too heavy anyway.

The Lonely Angry Hearts

Be kind to people who are angry.
They are finding a way to make it beautiful but it's hard.
Because anger sticks so nicely with the heart—giving
acknowledgment to everything they've been through,
when people didn't.

No Empaths In The Room

It's funny how this event was given one role of
victim,
no collateral is allowed.
No emotions valid from another side.
One role.

I try to give myself comfort by telling myself this
has been done before.
Jesus hanging on the cross…
Mary, guards—weeping.
how foolish.
Made in the image of God but this time I can't look
away.

Greedy

You and I
sitting face to face at the granite countertop, in my
new 70's home, writing memoirs of our trauma.
The lighting in the room is a beaming yellow tone
and it gives your skin a complementing glow.
You begin yours, and I glide my hand on top of
yours, holding it.
Not letting you go through it alone.
As I pick up the pen after you—glimmered in sweat
I go to begin mine.

But you grabbed the pen and wrote it for me.
Your grip was tight.
You wouldn't let go.
Until, I was on the floor. Sobbing.
You dropped the pen on the floor.
Bouncing against the wood right by my ear.
The pen was in 2 halves.
I couldn't change what you've done.
I had no eraser to edit the damage.
I just had to learn,
that some people write your story worse, to better their own.

I have not written a new story since.

Collateral Damage

He died for you in the beginning.
Your eyes saw him shove the knife in his own chest.
What I saw was different.
I died in the beginning.
I watched him draw back a dagger to put in you…
He missed and sunk it in me.
Someone needs victory in this fairytale.
I just don't remember auditioning for casualty.

Tag

I'm still here
In the hallway that I wasn't in,
being shoulder checked, ran right past by.
The worry of being caught was passed to me
like some game of tag.
I'm not there, I never was.
But now I'll forever be.

Melpomene

It's a tragedy…when only God and one human know the truth behind the innocent mask one puts on their face. Was that a tear that just hit the floor? I thought you were done pretending. Is it still everyone else's fault?

Lipstained Stationary

You roleplayed your trauma with me and prepped it on a platter and served it to me with a pretty white note that said "You did this to me. How dare you."

New God

How lucky for the new young girls that walk to that altar with no need to repent about the man right in front of them.
Bending her knees for what was at first for a Savior but then for one who created himself as one.
He wrote his own Ten Commandments, told her how loved and precious she was, then sent her to Hell.

Snow Globe

I'm unhealed and messy
Betrayed and sealed.
How can you hate me for living in a house you once did?
You may have locked it and thrown away the key.
But I stay in the closet with my box of copies by my feet,
with my face buried in my knees.
You flee from what happened,
I stay and hope if I do, I could possibly change what was done.
For you, you can look back as if just a memory.
But my chest is rising and falling in a frozen frame—
like a snow globe and it's snow.
It's alive in a place so still.

No one's here anymore.

Wax On The Floor

This sadness became my best friend. My lover.
I can't live without it. I sat hours binge eating its hunger.
I slept in bed with it.
Multiple times.
I cradled the shaking overwhelmed mess
I picked up the glass of thrown vases
And went to court to plead for its case.
I held its hair as it threw up the poison it abused.
I covered its eyes as it reread hate posts that didn't understand.
We broke up and it keeps calling me week after week.
Month after month. Haven't heard from it for awhile and it's my birthday now.
It blew out my candles for me.
How did we get here.
It used me. And now it hates me. Why do I still love you.

Sullen Mother

Elephant in the room.

It's no secret that I don't want to release this tragedy.

I didn't birth it myself but I adopted it, took it in as my

own.

I don't want this sadness to move out.

My Blade Now

I hear all the time "A bad person doesn't try to be better"...
so you are good!

I wish someone would tell me "You have full permission to be the bad guy." with how they've repeatedly stabbed you, you have full authority over the knife you pull out from the thickness of your muscle and get to use it however you'd like.

Better Person

Being the better person comes in waves. I'm so close to being the one to admit I was wrong and apologize for my actions at times...
But then I wake up from the dream of "If only it was that easy."
Because forgiving you doesn't change what you did, and forgiving you doesn't make you see the wrong you served.
And as badly as I want this war to end. It doesn't, till I have your head.
Like you ended up never leaving, in mine.

Tattooed Hearts

We became more than friends. Not in a romantic way nor like kin. More like soulmates that lost the desire to ruin themselves for the other yet if it came down to a duel we'd put an end to ourselves to let the other have a chance to live again. And still be angry with our choice.

Awaiting Rescue

I want to be missed.
Your feelings came over for a sleepover and
refused to go home.
They shared details of kissed necks and secret
sanctuaries.

A backyard shed, cars and church halls, full of hot
breath, leading to a confused girl and a fallen
church.
I was tripping over bodies trying to save it.
God doing what He does best, carrying us in His
hands, but I tripped a little too far, slipping off the
palm.
No one noticed.
Not even God.

Kikazaru

I think the trial was really against
the person you are, and the person you hurt—
with the person I thought you were and the
friend I was as the jury.
Jury does not reach verdict
and the judge speaks so softly, *"This court is
adjourned."*
Why did I cover my ears?
Why did my eyes have to be blinded by rage and
confusion, in salted secretion?
I think I do this to myself.
Never allowing an answer to fill the void.
the void gives me a space to breathe.

Cenotaph

I killed you off.
I finally did it.
I spent so long sharpening this knife of anger and rage.
Put it aside for another day.
The day came and I was filled with understanding and peace.
I quickly shoved the blade in your chest.
You are 6 feet under now.
Where you needed to be a long time ago.

I sat by your headstone.

longer than I should've.

Hypocrite

"Sometimes people choose to see the best and worst in people, and love them anyway.
Those are the best kinds of people."
I don't think the choosing has anything to do with the good or bad.
They saw my best and worst and didn't love me anyway.

What kind of person does that make them then?
"The worst?"
Yes.

But I fucking love them anyway.

Honey Creeks And Black Tea

Sympathy runs down my broken heart like honey at times.. as I remember, what happened, we went through together.
But then you take all the honey, time and time again.
Sweetening your black tea with it, just to spit it at my face.
Please stop taking the honey.
I'm running out and losing my taste for it.

Mosaic

                                                I'm hurt.

                                I'm mad. I'm not hurt.

                                I'm hurt. I'm not mad.

                                             I'm mad.

I don't think I could speak to you ever again.
If I saw you. I'd look right through you, because
you are now glass to me. Shattered pieces glued
together by forgiveness. Not for you. But for me.
You are nothing to me.

Sorry

I'm not the same person I used to be,
and I know you aren't either.
But the old me is still waiting for that apology
and the old you still struggles to be right.
My forgiveness isn't in my hands—

It's in theirs.

Healing Tug-A-War

I hate what you did to me,
but I loved who you were.
I hate what your hands fabricated,
but loved the way you did your nails.
I hate that you still did something wrong after,
but I love that you are now loved the way you
deserved all along.
I will hate you for the rest of my life I think,
but I'll always love the little hope I have inside me
that I will forgive you someday.

Stockholm Syndrome

Happy one year anniversary.
Do I hand you flowers through the bars?
I don't think I could let go of them—why are you smiling.

The Sky Wept

The day is creeping around the corner.
The anniversary where it rained and hasn't stopped since.
Some days it just sprinkles, just enough where the air dries it in a second.
others, it pours.
I know, no one will remember it like you.
But I will remember when, every time.
I set candles at night, memories lined up for recollection.
In memory of who we used to be but in honor of how you became free.
I don't blow out the flames because he might mistake it as his birthday.
I let it engulf my house in flames,
the rain is coming soon anyway—it always does in June.

Fast Car

I swore I saw your car pass me. Did the ghost of who
you were, wave at me?
I passed the car lot just to be sure, and there it was, a
new one in its spot
now it will haunt me for sure.

One Call Away

You know I was one call away for you to say sorry.
Even though you didn't want to admit to what you did over that beat up black plastic phone because someone else would hear—
I was one call away.
One call away for you to say the bond you had with me was real.
Was I just a part of the blueprint in the construction site to come for your new life to be built?
Of course.
It was easy.
How could you not?
I sat next to my phone waiting to accept the request, for months, and I bet all you did was sit and think about where in the blueprint was flawed.

Ghost Memories

It's like it never happened.
My memories turned into eraser dust and swiped off the table to clear off the page.
While another story is written in its place.
But
I still see the shadings of the story written before.
this story will never allow for a perfect white page again.
I think he would smile.
to know he left his mark
and that he made it permanent.
I guess that was just his thing.
darkening, then leaving it impossible to brighten.

April Showers

April has come.
I've yet to become quick at diffusing my anger when I think of you.
I've yet to become quick at forgetting all the vengeance that filled my thoughts for far too long.
or maybe long enough.

Wreckage

What if the airbag doesn't deploy.
What if everything I ever did and everything I didn't do, to go through what I did again was all meant for nothing because all I was designed for was wreckage.
I'm going to wreck aren't I?
"Every good thing must come to an end"
But what if I was never good?
This will never end.

I wish I was good.

You Win

I have a game of Jenga blocks stacked in my body of words I want to say.

I pull each phrase carefully to say what I actually mean without crumbling everything I've built.
I may be fragile but it's only because others have been so careless—they don't mind to start again.
I swear to god if this fucking falls-
She has this dream of running through flowers in the hills of California.
letting sun rays hit her iris, one eye squinted shut

from the shine.
the breeze rushing through the strands that
lift off her neck.
But,
My legs are getting itchy,
I hate that I had to lend you my sunglasses
and I'm envious of how long your hair has
gotten, we cut it at the same time but mine
hasn't budged an inch.

Wet Shoes

I still count my breaths to ignore the past from
flooding my thoughts.
I swallow every memory with a bad taste like a shot,
so the burn doesn't last too long.
I scream at bad drivers from the barrier of steel,
just so I can relieve some pressure from my chest.

but I see y'all doing well
and it truly makes me glad.
I wish I could still lift my hands in surrender.
I wish I could laugh about the good times I'm living
in, now that I'm healed.
but instead, my

therapy works at the sort of speed that feels
like when you run in a dream.
or like
when you are staring at the massive puddle in
front of you, in the way of where you are
going but you can't possibly wet these shoes.
I don't go anywhere.
I'm stuck on the side of the road where I
first heard the bad news and I'm still waiting
to walk away the same person

but I can't possibly wet these shoes.

21st Birthday

It's my 21ST and all I'm worried about is the ghost that I haven't seen in awhile. The haunting of our falling doesn't show up as much as it used to and I hate that I miss the fright.
I hate that I don't have to fight anymore.
I miss throwing the punches. I miss the creases between my eyebrows and the trails of black from my eyes.
I don't want to get through it. I don't want to be passed it. behind me. out of reach.
I can handle being over it. Casually sitting beneath. Underneath. Where I can glance down every once in a while and add a drop of liquid to the river of sorrow.
It's my 21ST and I'm walking backwards to do just that.

Pacifier

I lost my baby boys first pacifier today in Santa Monica.
I retraced my steps, checked the streets, grieved it like it was all that mattered to me.
Reminded me of you.
Because what happened to you, the way you were lost—
I could've sworn I didn't go too far. If someone were to ask, I'd know exactly where you are.
I questioned how well I knew you at all.
The self talk in your head, the company you kept.
They sent me; a search party of one into empty woods because you've already moved on.
I retraced my steps, checked the streets, grieved you like what happened to you was all that mattered to me.

We Should Cut Off Our Fingers

Casting out demons
praising a Savior
to
pointing our fingers
and giving reason to our misbehavior.
You were my laugh keep safe.
When hurt comes in to steal joy, we become
thieves ourself, becoming the hurt to someone
else.
And we did just that.
Even if peace came,
because the absence of our joy, we couldn't help
retuning back to pointing our fingers and giving
reason to our misbehavior.
I miss casting out demons and praising a savior.

Reminiscence

Today I'm past it. Today I remember you as my friend. My sister without you after blood.

Small Town American Girl Version

Annalise, sweet Anna.
I wish you let someone know the version he was telling you—
    the Lord said tangled in sheets before 18 wasn't the best idea before a ring.

Neither is a cold room with no windows hidden away from truth.
How'd he trick your kind mind to ever convincing you of such things.

He sat on the other side of the confessional, smirking knowing your inveterate journey.
Living in a Morse code, he created a new language.
He was sick, he was twisted, he made baggage.
Forgiveness wasn't made for him.
Now she's living day to day re-writing her new story.
but no one sees the crack in the binding of the small town American girl version.

N Chris Street

You should remember me.
The way I would hold your heart in my hands, maybe too firm sometimes but it was only to protect.
I didn't mean to be a standing guard at your bedroom door,
I just didn't know if your mind was telling you rescue would be forever with him instead.
If you knew then what you do now, would we still be friends?
Would you still cover the skeletons in my closet with my clothes we would share, as I did yours?

Would we still be laughing over my kitten going wild in the kitchen?
Would the shutter of the camera still be echoing the field as our creativity bloomed?
I'm still wondering if guarding you was my only mistake… I don't wish that to be true.
Should I just have waited in the car, as a getaway when you were ready?
Would you have slipped away through the backyard,
back into his arms, if so?

Blow Out My Fire Too

If you weren't a black used match—finally cooled off and I; a match still on fire running up the hand that holds it, I think we would be great friends again.

Trauma Bond

It's my 22nd.
I think we would make great friends now.
I think our tears watered enough the seeds of
empathy, but we still hold on to the sensitive three
year old we birthed together.
we never really discussed coparenting.
and warmth still gives me chills.
I have a guard dog by the fence I built myself. she
only growls at smiling faces, words of assurances and
kind touches.
I can't trust, still.
not the white picket fence I dreamt about.
I wonder what house you've built for yourself.
how are you protecting your child?
It's my 22nd.
and I'd think we'd be great friends now.

To The Victim

I believe you.
Fully.
I will never understand but as I piece together the puzzle of the secret mess you were forced to live in.
My empathy grows.
My eyes open with each sliver of light you let out of the room you stay in with the door shut with your back against it.
You are good.
I believe you. Fully.
I will never understand but my lips curve as I see you standing back up after hiding with your head to your knees in your skin after so long.

Hey you.

I'm proud of your voice. Even if it was just a whisper. Even if it was a crack.

I saw your eyes scream for help as you talked about how your food made you feel at lunch.

As you played in survival mode, I played the toughest game of I spy looking for a rope to pull you out of the quicksand you didn't notice you walked in years ago.

Crash Your Party

I'm sorry I can't be there for your 21st birthday party.
It feels like it was only yesterday that you were blowing
out 18 candles.

I went out to get streamers and came back to someone else
planning your party.
I could not find my name on the guest list.
I did not wear black tie…
since when do you wear black tie?
And it's not that I didn't want to go,
there was just simply no room.
I wish it was as simple as "growing apart" but we both
know that isn't true.

because we both cry to the same songs in our car, miles apart.
and there are still streamers in my closet.

There are still streamers in my goddamn closet.

Dirty Hands

The connection between mentors
feelings of inclusion and love
The learner of new things and thinking it's more than
being a part.
Starting a family, not of blood but bread and wine.
I envy the new lives of the youth that walk through
those doors
because
I pray they never know what it was like—
to watch it crumble so fast,
to be torn apart
becoming evidence and whispers over

what was done, in every hallway of
stained glass.
nothing was the same
no prayer or hands laid.
no miracle. no faith.
could save me the pain I felt since that
day.
But my hope for you is different.
I pray your savior stays God—

Everybody Dies

I see the building of your secrets.
The same ones you used your prophecies for.

I don't see the walls anymore that I used to worship between.
But I remember how it felt. To know I was safe and on holy ground.
You
You took her and made her your god,
worshiped her between those walls as she was unsure of the religion she was following — the cult you were creating.
You took holy ground and left holes in her memory.
She wasn't supposed to grow up this fast.
You killed her as a child and raised a new body that knew yours as the mother.

When the nurse told you to do skin to skin
did you know yours would be poison to
hers? Melt her slowly till she was nothing.
No no, it didn't bother
you
let the epidermis of your fingertips glide
across her eyelids.
I bet her eyelashes were soft.
I bet her heart was still good.
I bet you didn't know The one and only
God was preparing for her resurrection.
I bet you didn't know He was rebuilding
what you destroyed.
The nurse was fired.
The hospital received an eviction notice.
Three years later I think her eyes opened
quite nicely.
Not from the help of you

Not anymore.

Your Silence Is Mine

The only forgiveness you get is the pause before I share a little more than I should.
The curiosity of intentions behind every person who shows interest in being my friend—before I invite someone into my home.
You don't get my words, and you don't get to give me yours.

 I don't need them.

I already carry the silence of three years, you gave me after you went quiet from what was done and I had to live my life with no choice but to not understand why.
I had to live.
I had to carry silence in my pocket, and it was so full.
I had no space to carry anything else for three years.
So no.

You don't get my words.
And to what?
To just be crossed off your list of wrongdoing to move on from guilt?
No you keep that.
You keep that in your pocket, and you let it grow.
Till your pockets hang low and drag against the floor.
Let it calcify
 and scrap the ground,
till it digs your grave
because the version of myself that sang hallelujah had to die.
But I lived.
So all you get is the high wall I've built to protect me from anyone that could love me and pray for my salvation.
All you get is the 10 seconds I have to stop and breathe in and out when I remember I lost everything I loved.
    You don't get my words and I don't want yours.